W… ss!

by **Barbara Mitchelhill**
illustrated by **Michael Reid**

“Gran is coming,” said Mum.

“Good,” said Hope.

She liked Gran.

“Gran can sleep in the little bedroom,”
said Hope.
But the little bedroom was in a mess.

"Let's do up the little room!" said Mum.
"Yes!" said Hope.

They went to the shop. They got paint and wallpaper. They got curtains and a lamp.

Harvey and Carl wanted to put up the wallpaper. They made a mess.

The cat got in the paint. It made a mess.

Harvey and Carl wanted to help with the cake. They made a mess.

They put the cake on the table.
It looked good. They all liked it.

Harvey, Carl and Hope had a bath.
But they made a mess.

“Here’s Gran,” said Dad.

Hope wanted Gran to see the cake.

“Come and see what we did for you,” she said.

They went to look at the cake. Gran liked it.

“Did you do this for me?” she said.

“Yes we did,” said Hope.

They went to look at the little bedroom.
"Did you do this for me?" said Gran.
"Yes, we did," said Hope.

“Look at me!” said Gran.

“You look like the lamp!” said Hope.

“You look like the curtains!” said Harvey.

“Come on, Gran,” said Hope, “let’s go and have the cake.”

“Yes,” said Gran, “I like cake.”

“Oh no! Look what the cat did!” said Hope.

“What a mess!” said Gran.